HORSE — 30 MILES (48 KM) PER HOUR

SKATEBOARD — 15 MILES (24 KM) PER HOUR

DOG — 20 MILES (32 KM) PER HOUR

SPEEDBOAT — 150 MILES (241 KM) PER HOUR | NOW THAT'S FAST!: SPEEDBOATS

JACKRABBIT — 45 MILES (72 KM) PER HOUR

HUMAN — 12 MILES (19 KM) PER HOUR

BICYCLE — 15 MILES (24 KM) PER HOUR

NOW THAT'S FAST!
SPEEDBOATS

KATE RIGGS

CREATIVE EDUCATION

Published by Creative Education
P.O. Box 227, Mankato, Minnesota 56002
Creative Education is an imprint of
The Creative Company
www.thecreativecompany.us

Book and cover design by Blue Design
(www.bluedes.com)
Art direction by Rita Marshall
Printed in the United States of America

Photographs by Corbis (Wolfgang Deuter/
zefa, Mimi Mollica, Neil Rabinowitz),
Dreamstime (Deadandliving, Oscar1319,
Sugarfoot), Getty Images (China Photos, Fox
Photos, ROBERT FRANCOIS/AFP, Sandra Mu,
Andy Newman/Florida Keys News Bureau),
iStockphoto (Guntars Rakitko, Andrew
Ward)

Library of Congress Cataloging-in-
Publication Data
Riggs, Kate.
Speedboats / by Kate Riggs.
p. cm. — (Now that's fast!)
Includes index.
Summary: A quick-paced, colorful
description of the physical characteristics,
purposes, early history, and high-speed
capabilities of speedboats—some of the
fastest watercraft in the world.
ISBN 978-1-58341-915-1
1. Motorboats—Juvenile literature. I. Title.
II. Series.

GV835.R54 2009
797.12'5—dc22
2009002756

First Edition
9 8 7 6 5 4 3 2 1

A speedboat is a boat with a strong **engine**. The engine helps the speedboat go fast in the water. Most speedboats can go faster than 150 miles (241 km) per hour!

If a speedboat has more than one engine, it can go even faster

Speedboats are mostly used for racing. People like to race speedboats on rivers, lakes, and oceans. Most speedboats are not very tall. They sit low on the water.

SPEEDBOATS

Many speedboats are small. Only one person can ride in them. Other speedboats can hold a **crew** of four or five people. Speedboats are made of a strong material called fiberglass. Many boats are 30 to 50 feet (9–15 m) long.

Some speedboats have closed tops and look like race cars

The driver controls where the speedboat goes. He or she sits in the **cockpit**. The crew also sits in the cockpit. They help the driver take care of the boat. A speedboat is not very wide. Most speedboats have a front that is shaped like the letter *v*.

Speedboats in a race are marked with numbers on their sides

The first speedboat race was in 1904. It was held on a river in the state of New York. The boat that won the race went 25 miles (40 km) per hour. People thought that was really fast! But soon, people made speedboats go even faster.

This early speedboat from the 1930s was called the "Empire Day"

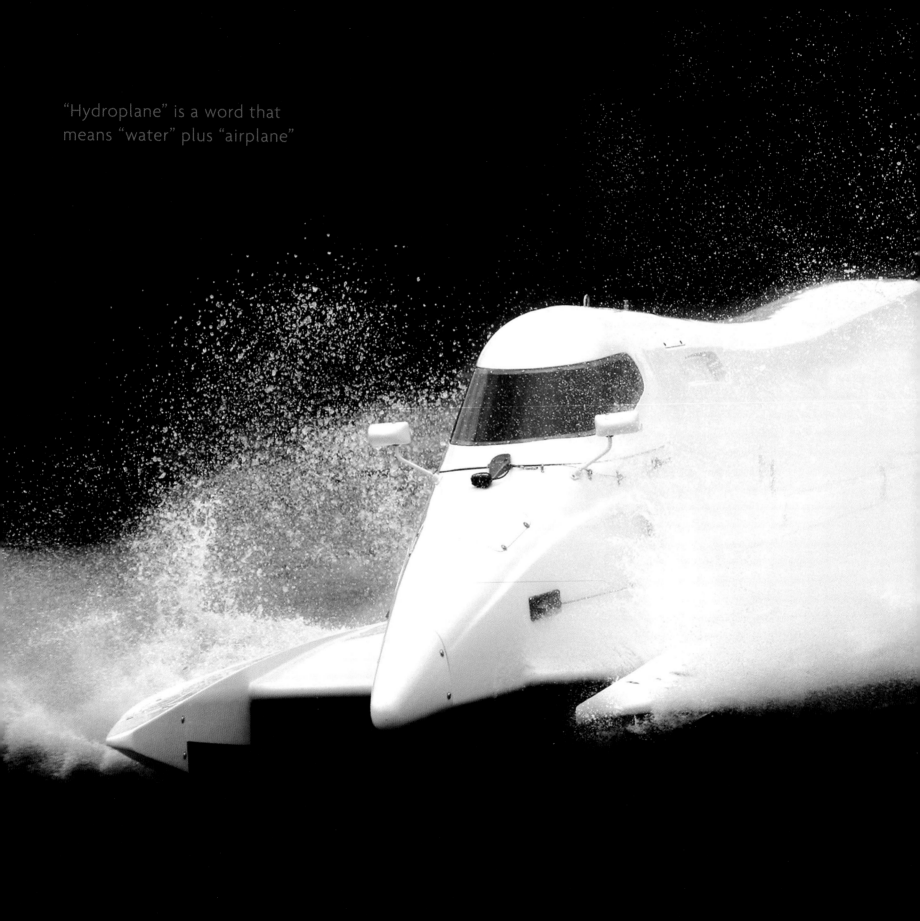

"Hydroplane" is a word that
means "water" plus "airplane"

Big speedboats called go-fast
boats have room for more people
to ride. But smaller speedboats
called hydroplanes carry only the
driver. Hydroplanes look a lot like
today's airplanes.

Hydroplanes have two parts on the sides called sponsons (*SPAHN-suhns*). These parts help the boat float on top of the water. A hydroplane can zoom across the water at 170 miles (274 km) per hour!

When a fast boat takes a tight turn, it sprays water everywhere

When speedboats race, they follow a long, straight **course**. Their engines roar as they slice through the water. The water sprays up behind the fast-moving boats.

Speedboats have to go straight so they do not run into each other

21

Speedboat drivers like racing their fast boats. They hold on tightly to the steering wheel and race their boats to the finish!

Fast Facts

Hydroplanes can reach very fast speeds because they barely touch the water.

Strong metal bars called a roll cage hold the cockpit together and keep the driver safe.

All boats have a part called the hull. This is a name for the main body of the boat.

Speedboat drivers have to pass a lot of safety tests before they can race other drivers.

Glossary

cockpit—the place where the driver sits in a speedboat

course—a path that something takes

crew—a group of people who work on a vehicle to make it run

engine—a machine inside a vehicle that makes it move

Read More about It

Hofer, Charles. *Speedboats*. New York: PowerKids Press/Rosen Publishing Group, 2008.

Sautter, Aaron. *Speedboats*. Mankato, Minn.: Capstone Press, 2007.

Web Site

Speedboat Coloring Page
http://www.coloring.com/color/speedboat
This page has a picture that can be colored online.

Index